email pbeneforti@gmail.com
personal website www.paolobeneforti.it
twitter: https://twitter.com/paolobitwo
facebook: https://www.facebook.com/paolobenefortiarte
Pinterest: https://www.pinterest.com/paolobitwo/work-of-art/
instagram: https://instagram.com/pbeneforti/

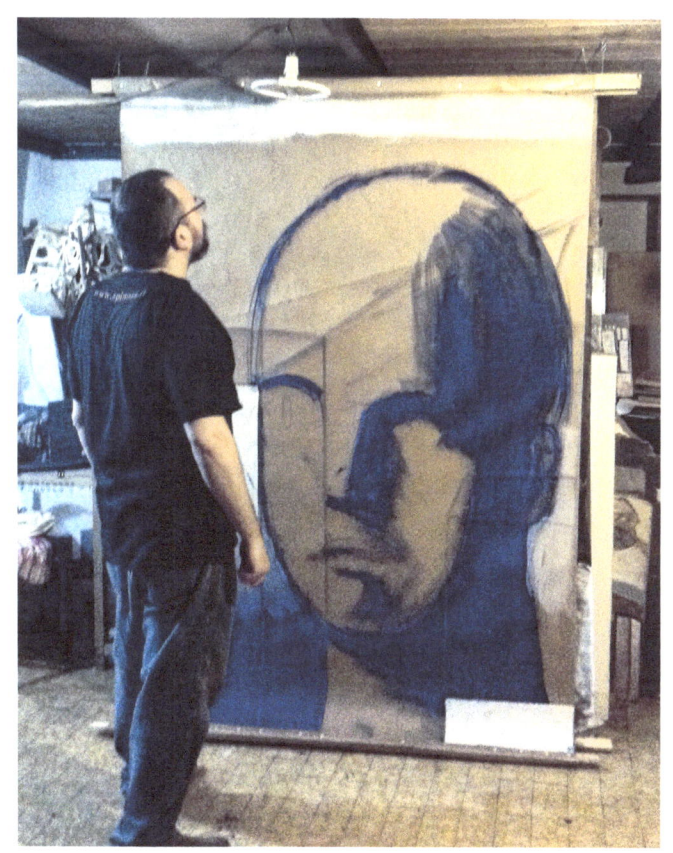

Paolo Beneforti

Solo exhibition
at Jordi Miguel Galeria d'Art in Barcelona
and other recent artworks

JORDI MIGUEL GALERIA D'ART
Bulevard dels Antiquaris 55-57,
Passeig de Gràcia, Barcelona
Web www.jmgaleria.tk
September 8-22
2016

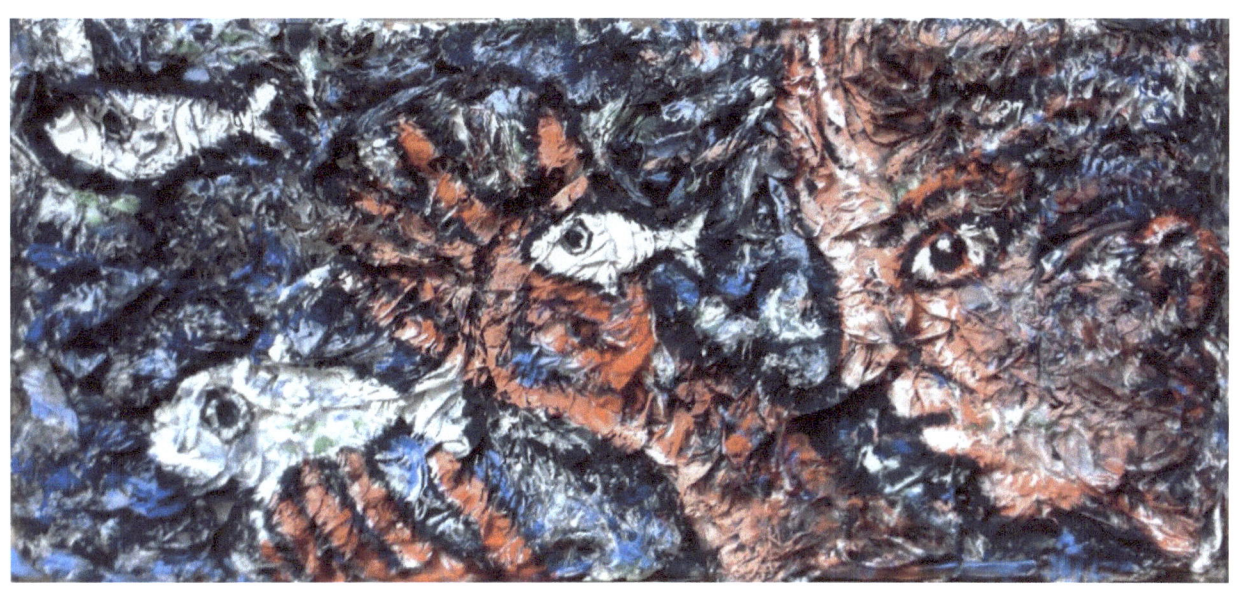

Fish hunter, gouache on crumpled paper, 2016

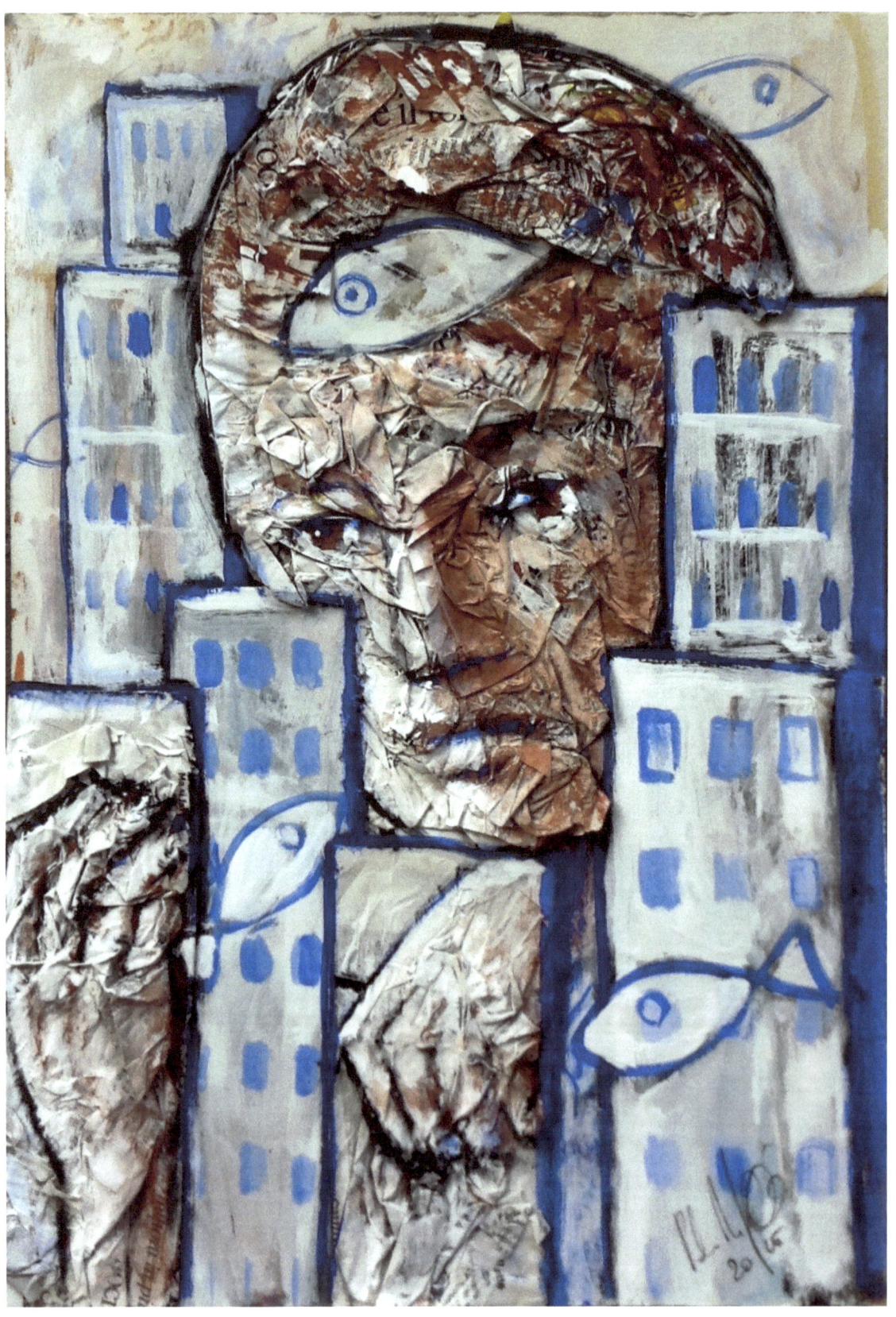

In the previous page: **With bare hands**, gouache and crumpled paper on cardboard

Below: **Many places**, collage and gouache on paper

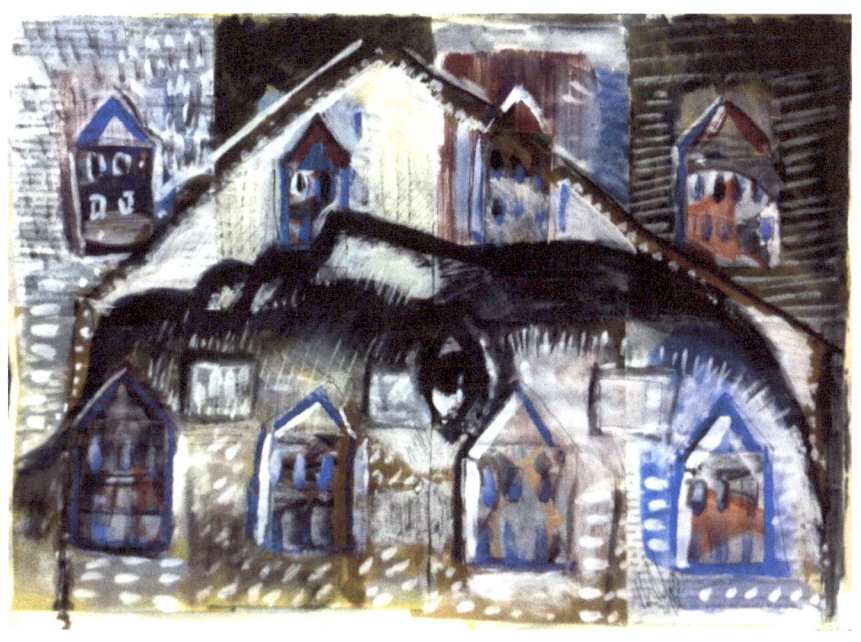

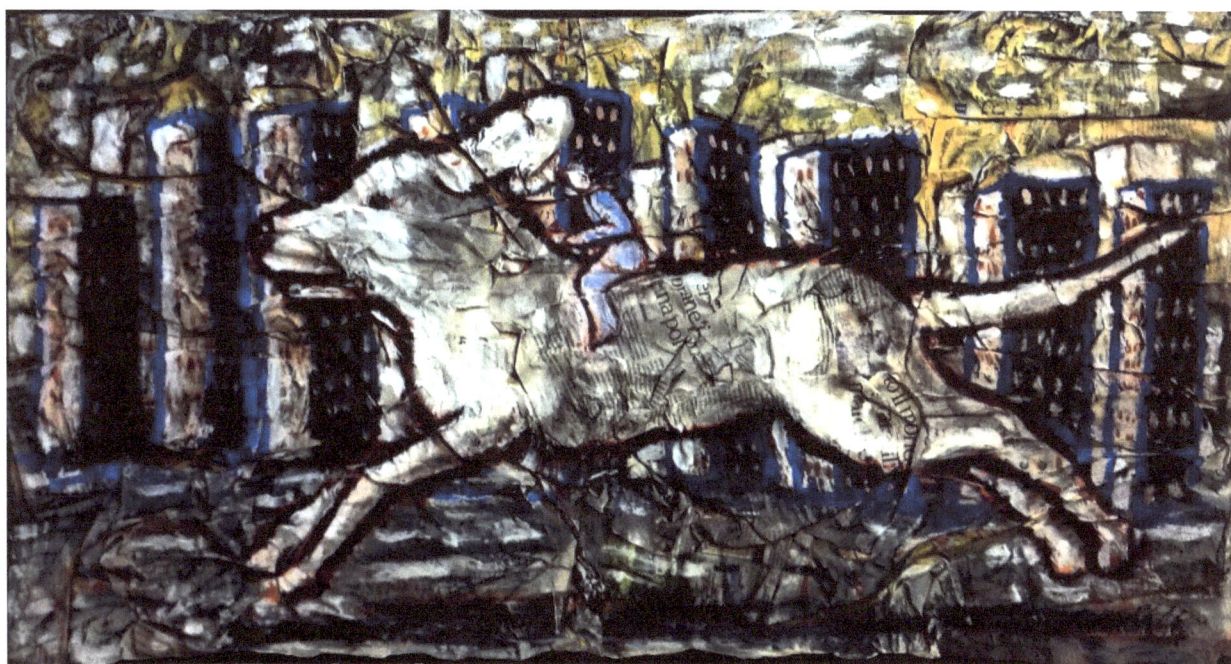

"Take me away!", gouache and crumpled paper on canvas

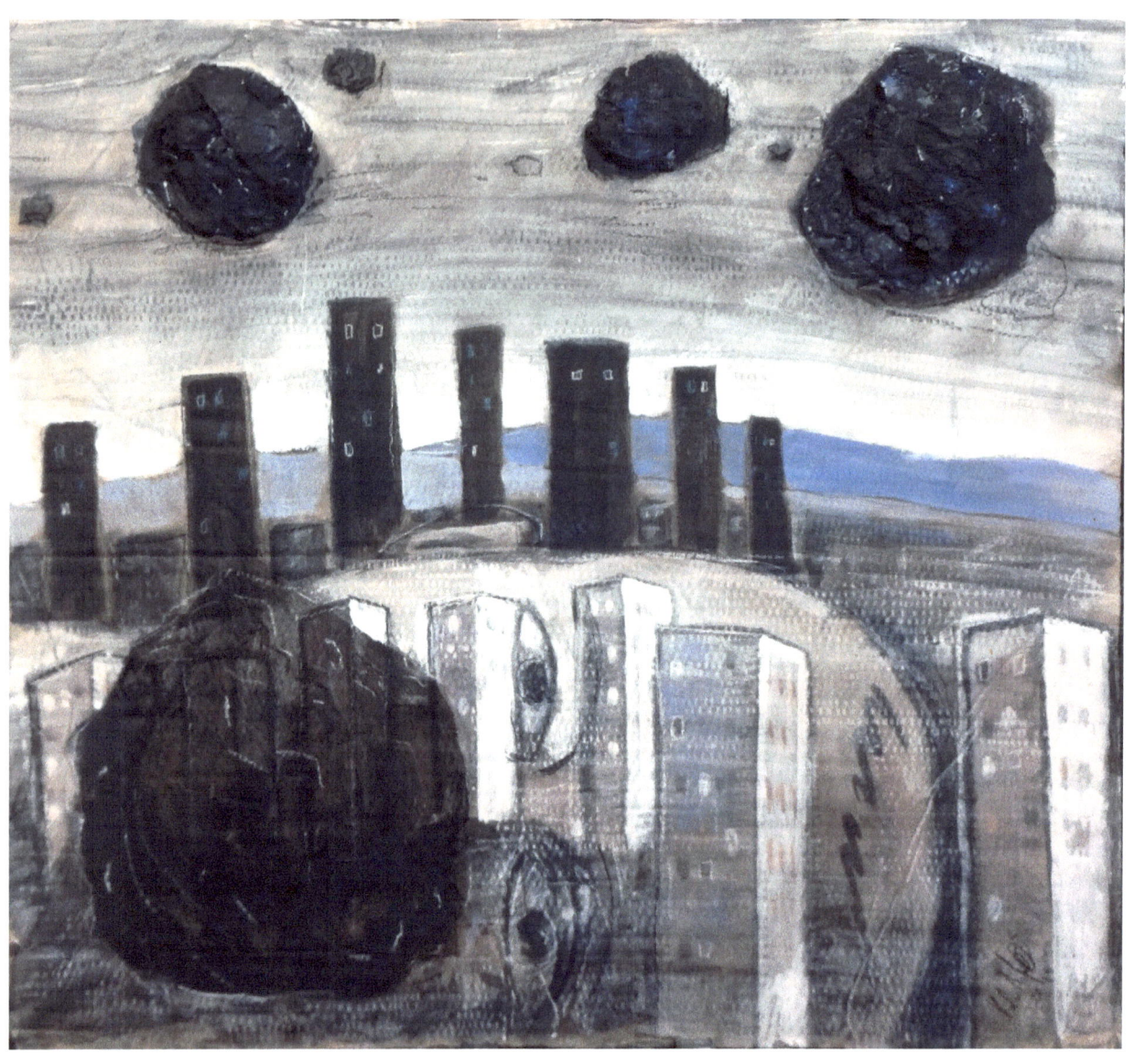

Black rain, gouache and paper on cardboard,

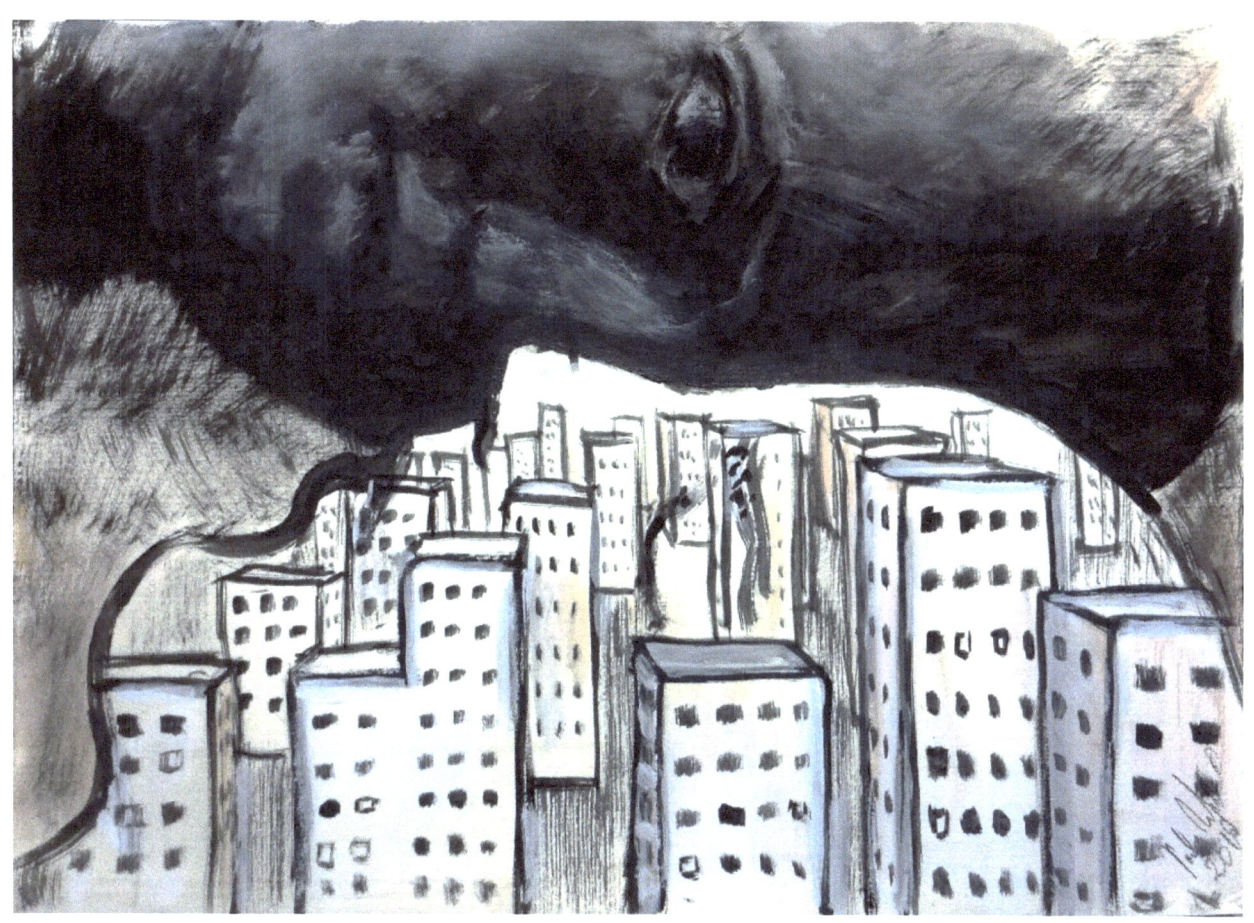

The naked city, gouache on paper

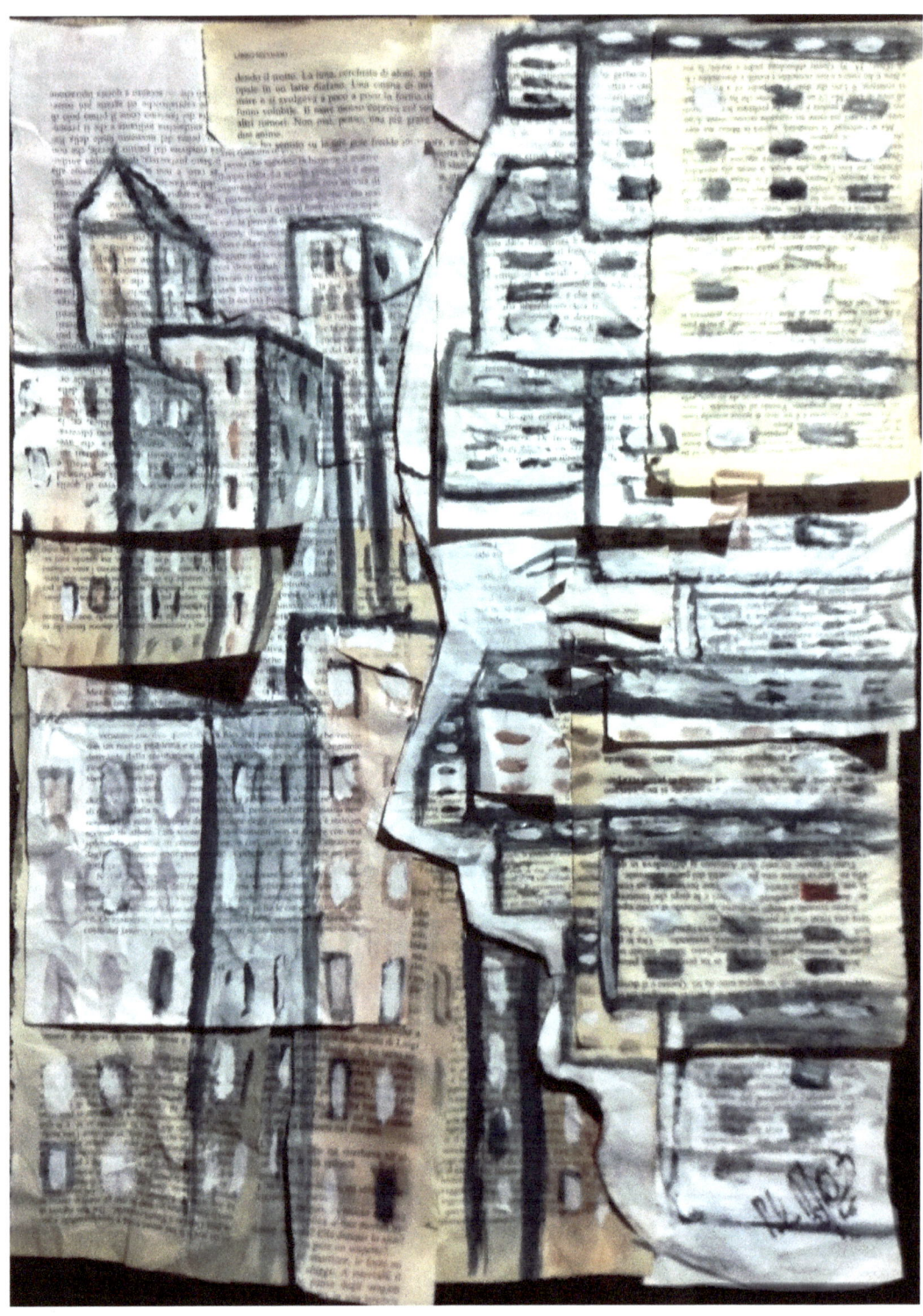

Wrong way, *gouache on crinkled book pages*

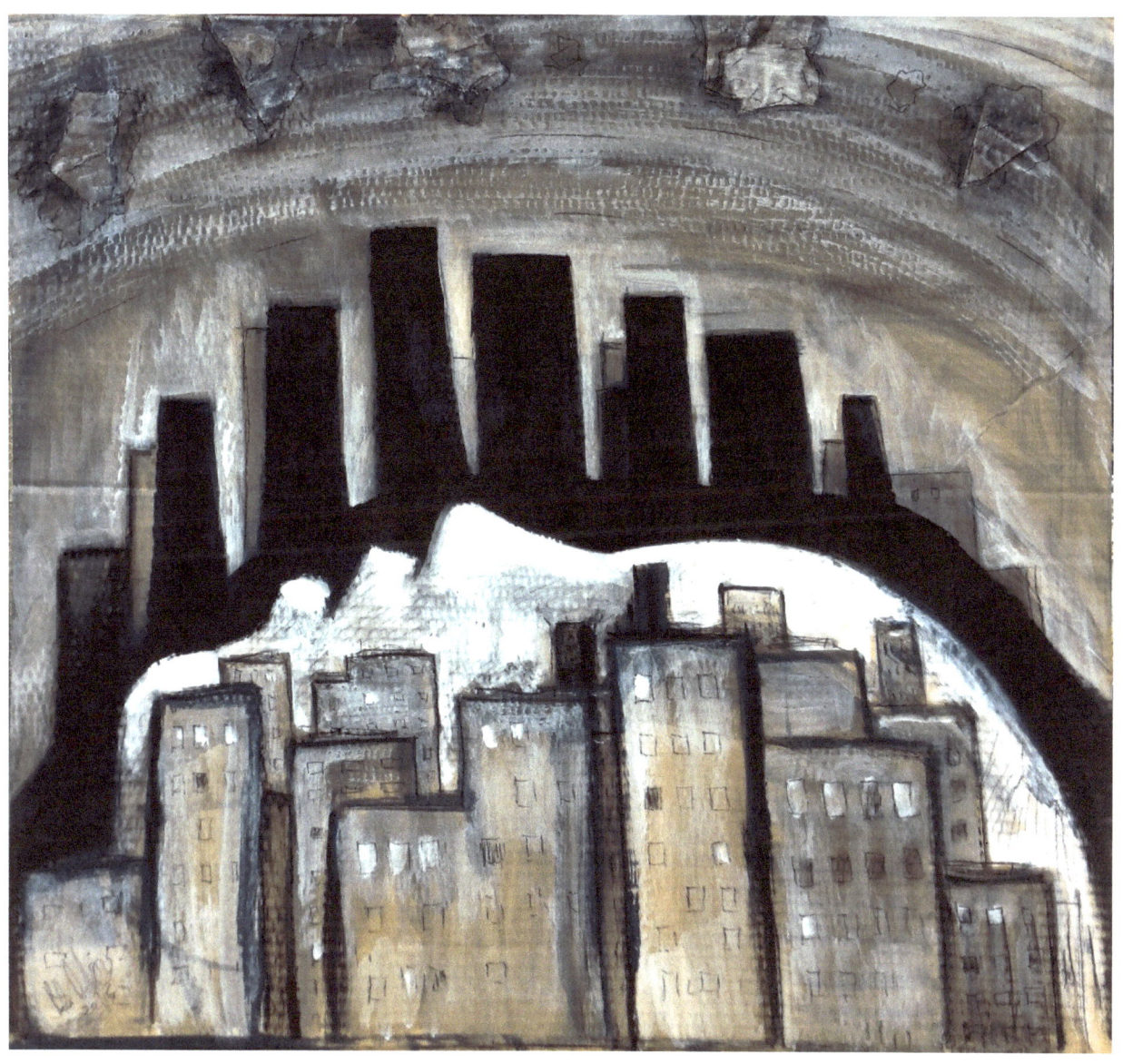

Starry night, gouache on cardboard

In the next page: *Windows*, gouache on paper, cm 150x220

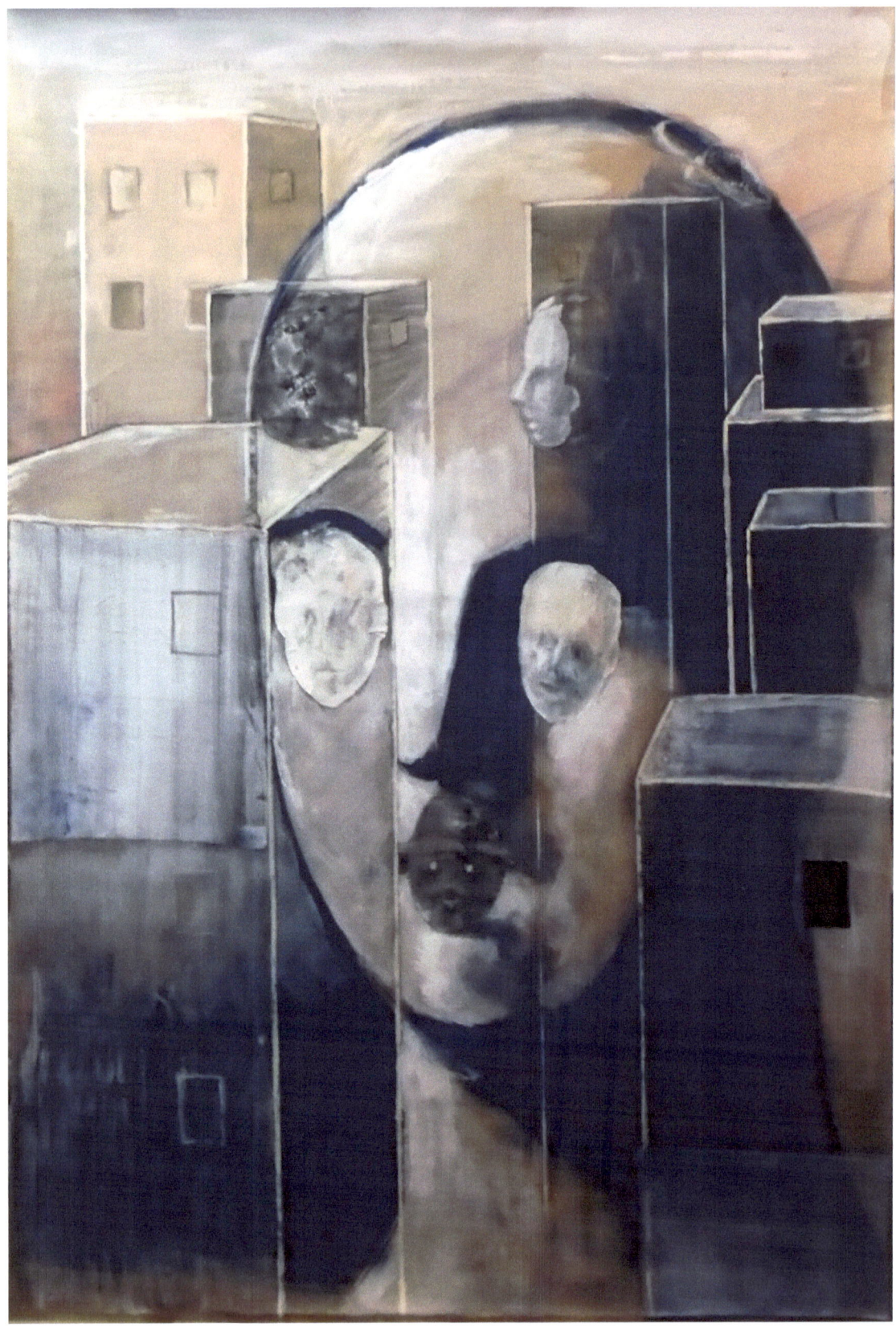

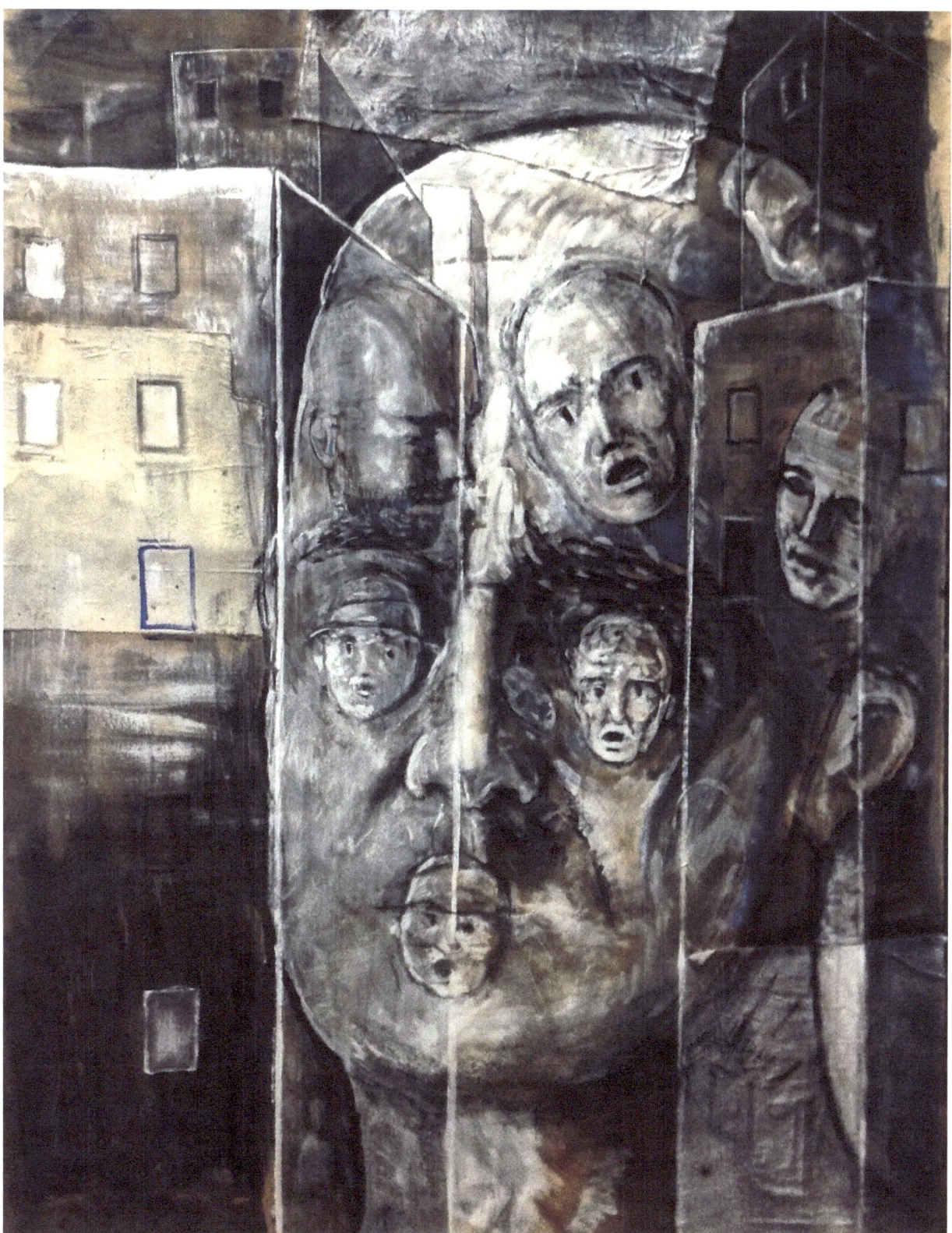

In the previous page: ***Many windows***, gouache on paper, cm 150x190

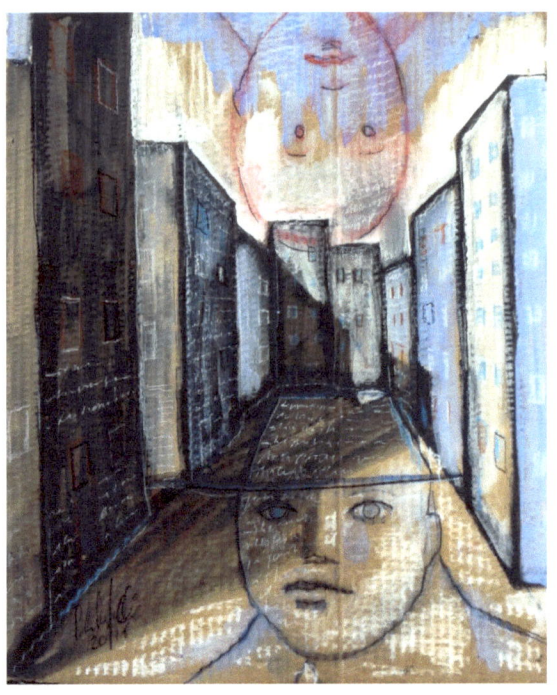

Built written. Gouache on recycled cardboard

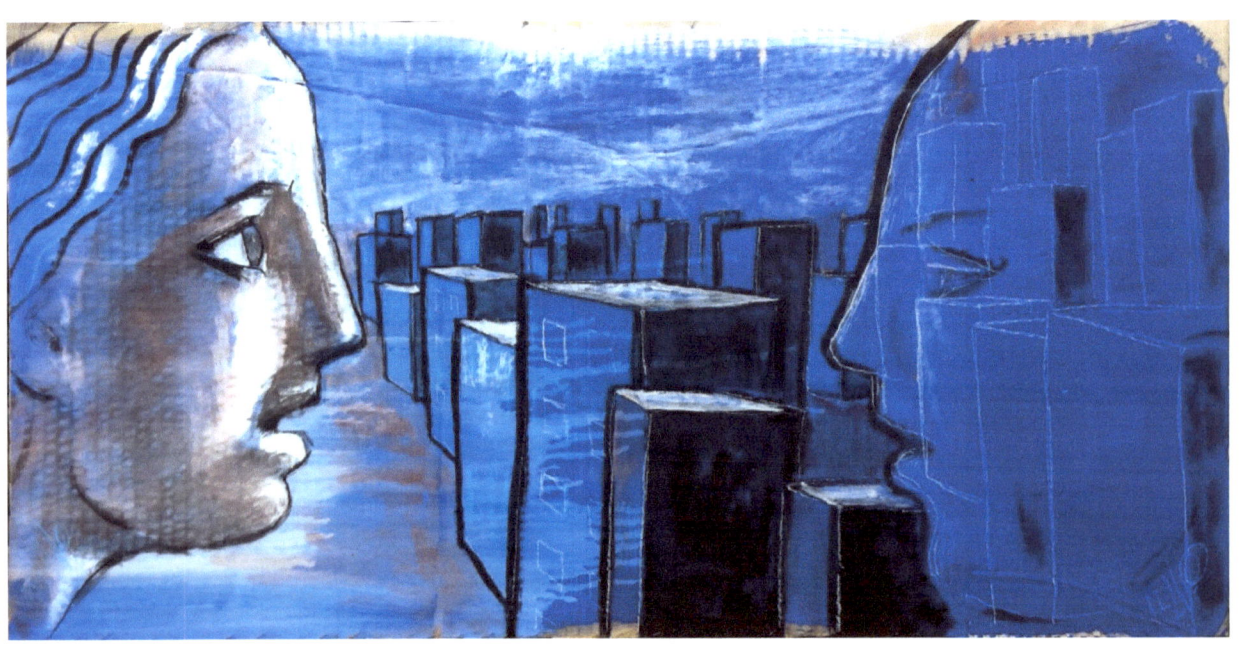

Teach me! Gouache on recycled cardboard

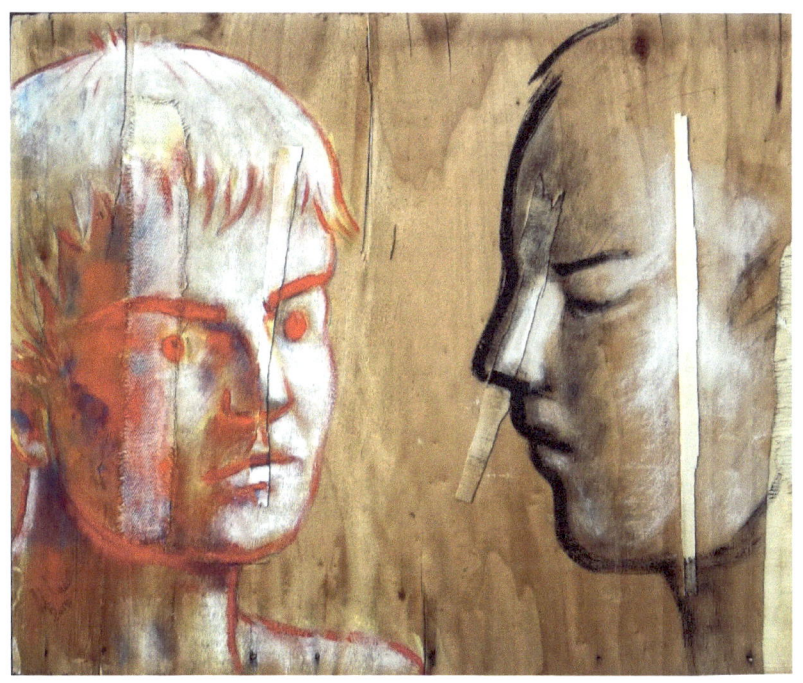

We'll fight. Gouache on wood

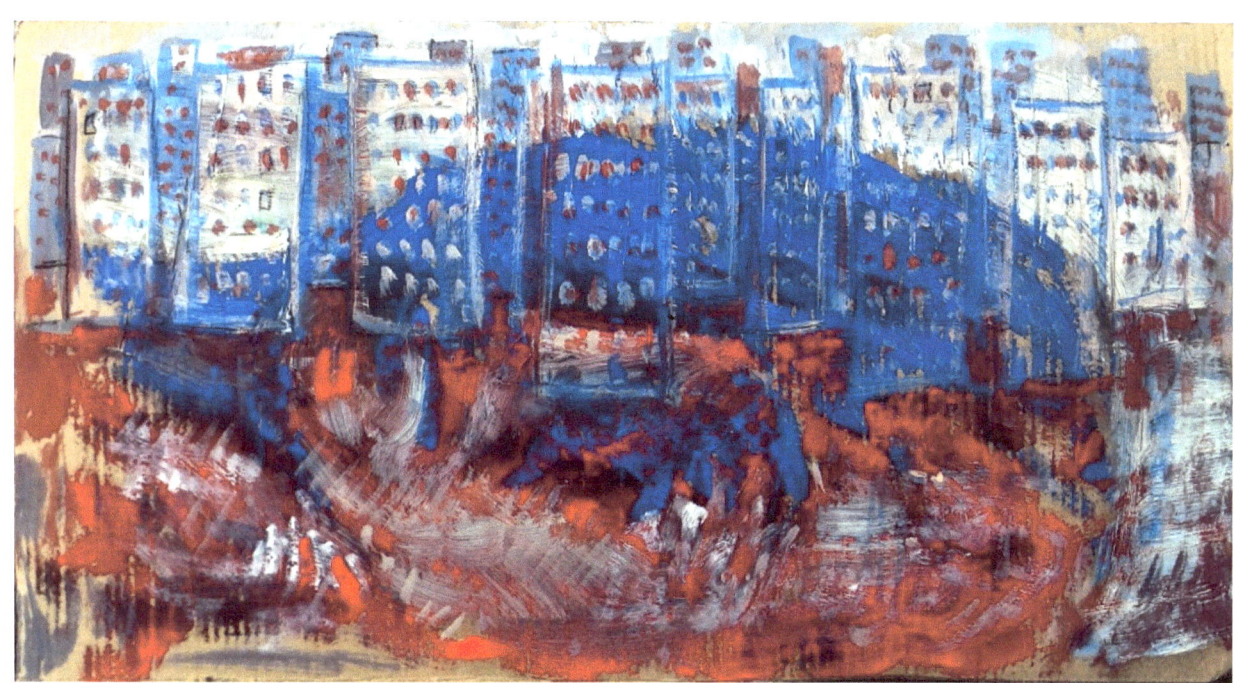

Dream of a city, oil on cardboard

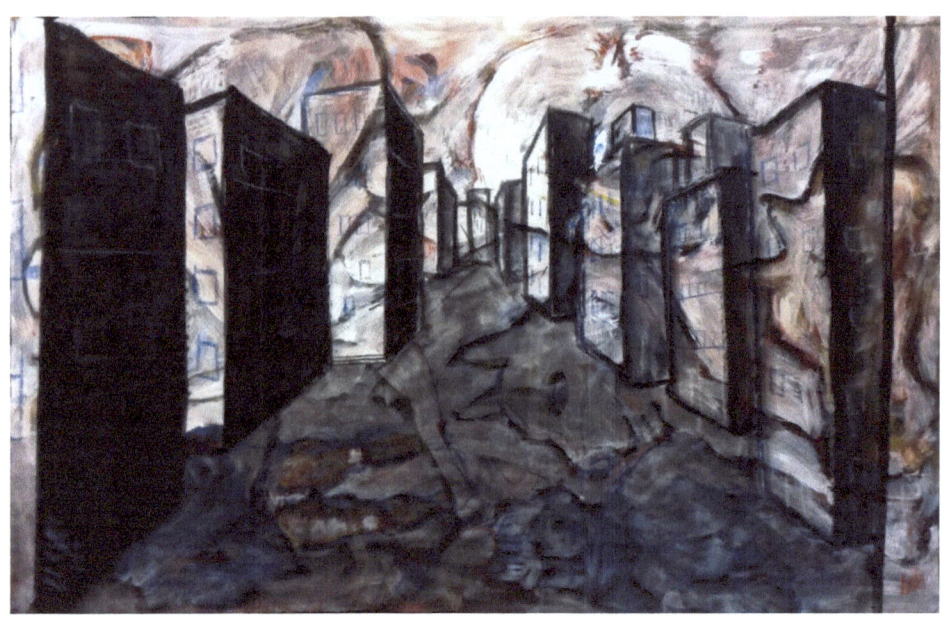

Tell me a story, gouache on cardboard

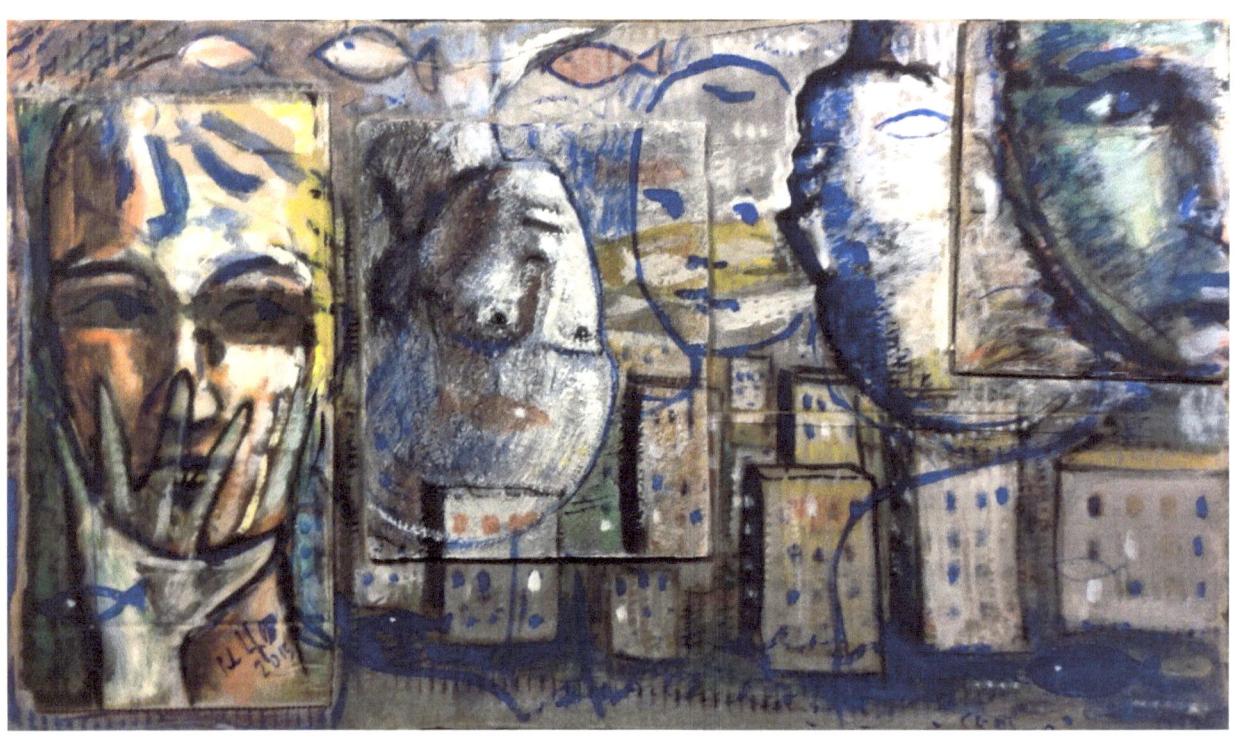

Mixed crowd, gouache on composite cardboard, 2015

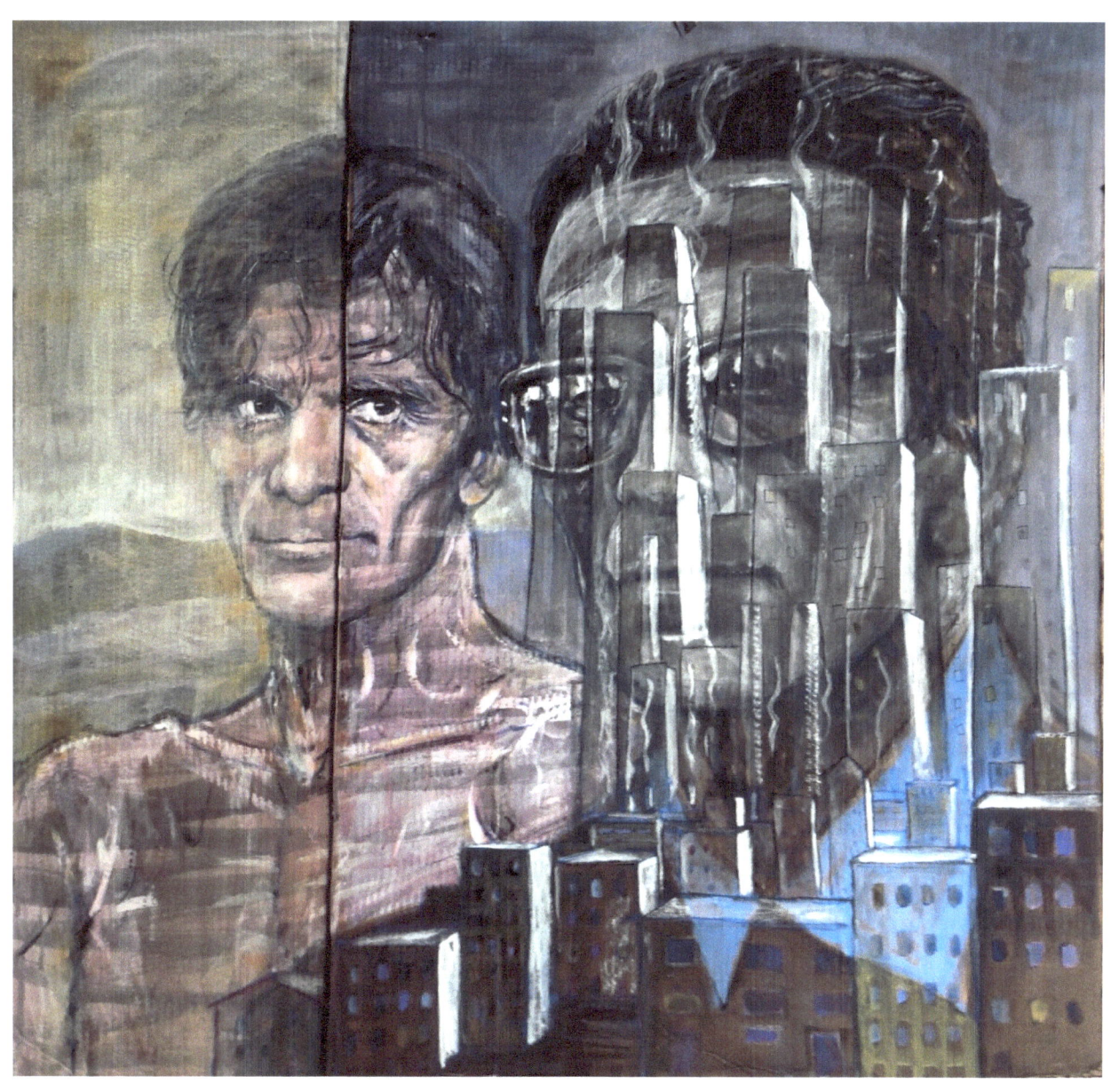

Double Pasolini, gouache on cardboard, cm 120x112

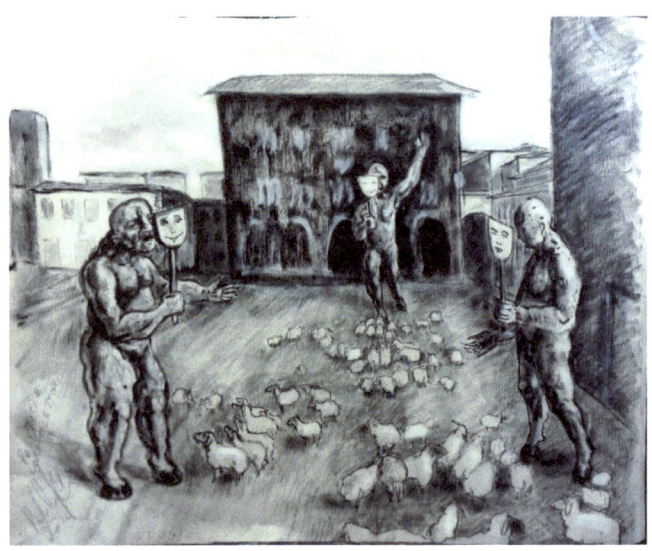

Politics, gouache on paper, 2015

Below: **Civic watch**, oil on cardboard

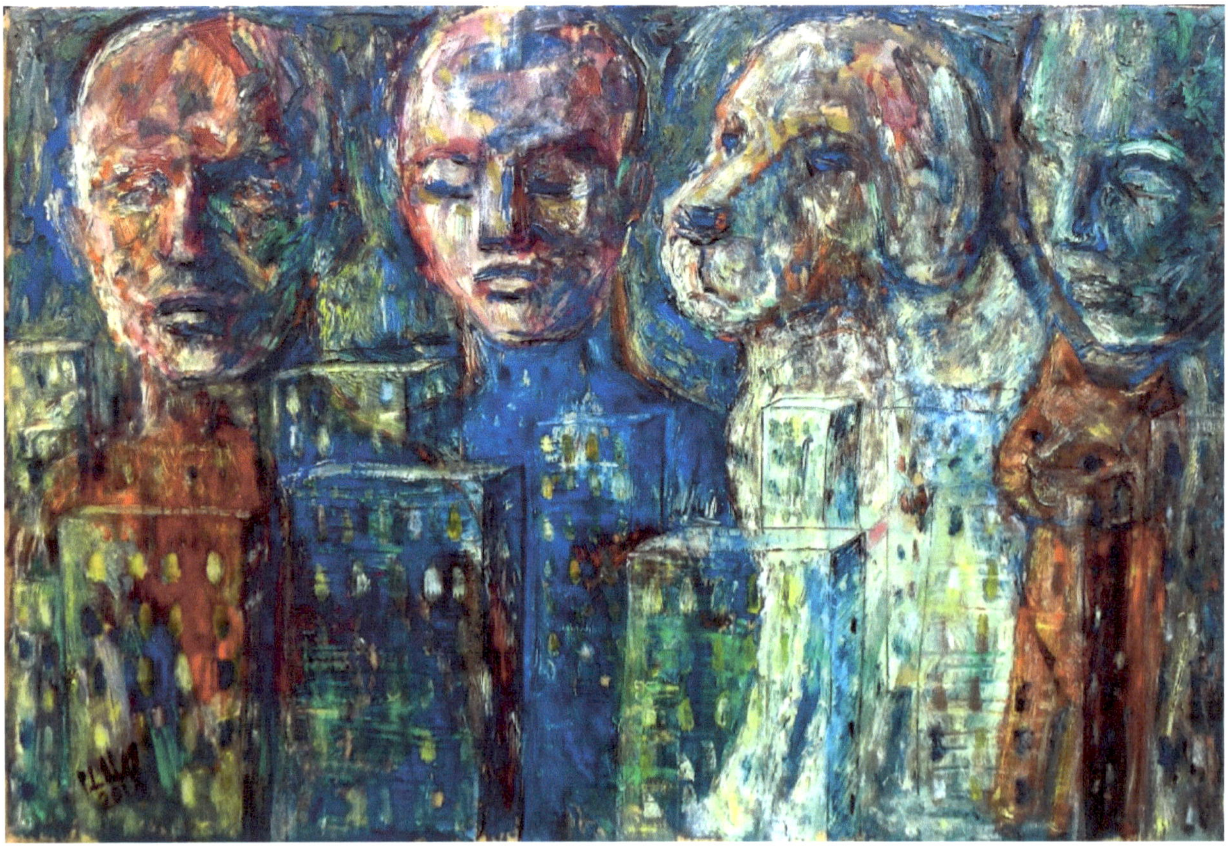

In the next page, **Many windows**, gouache and pastels on cardboard

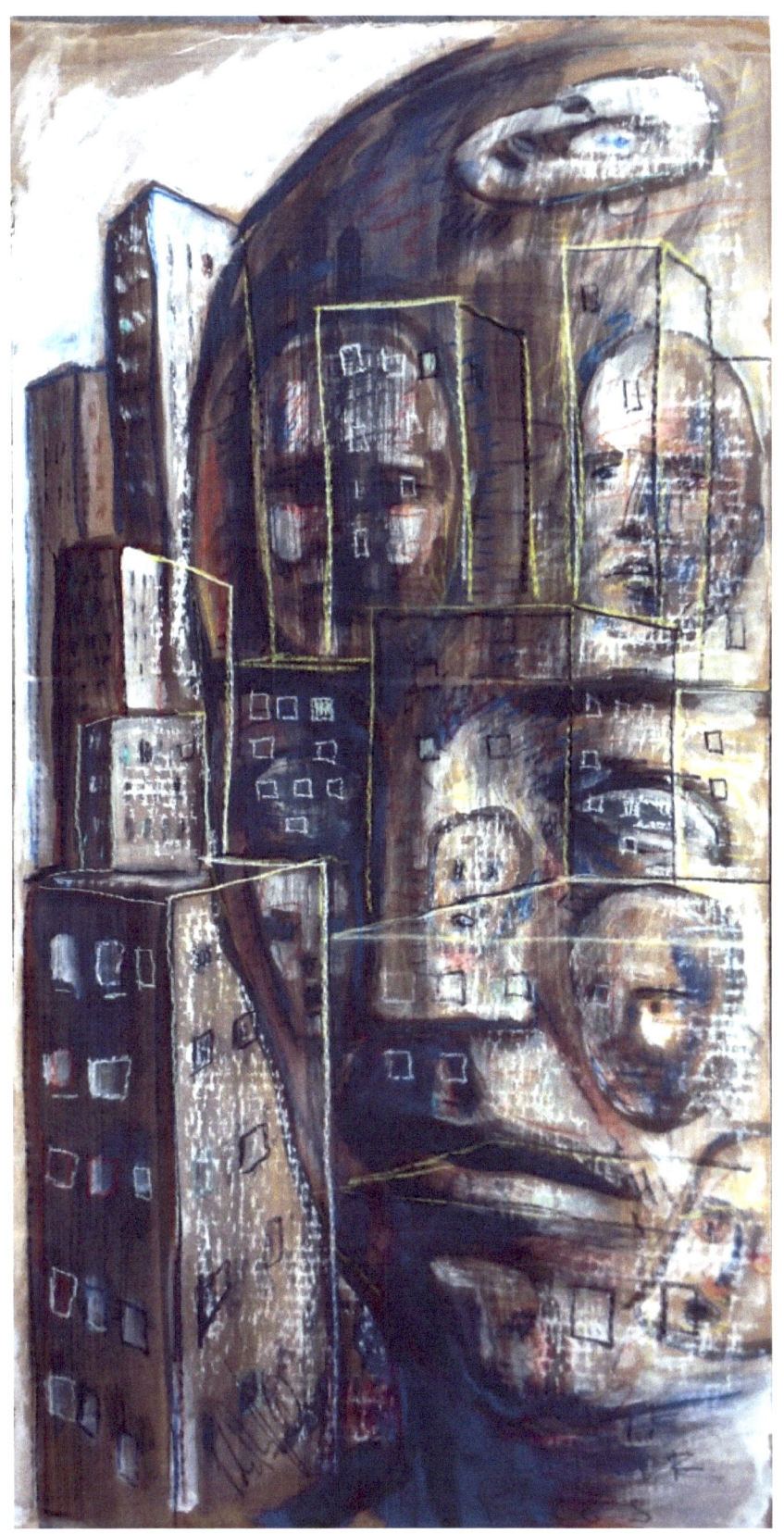

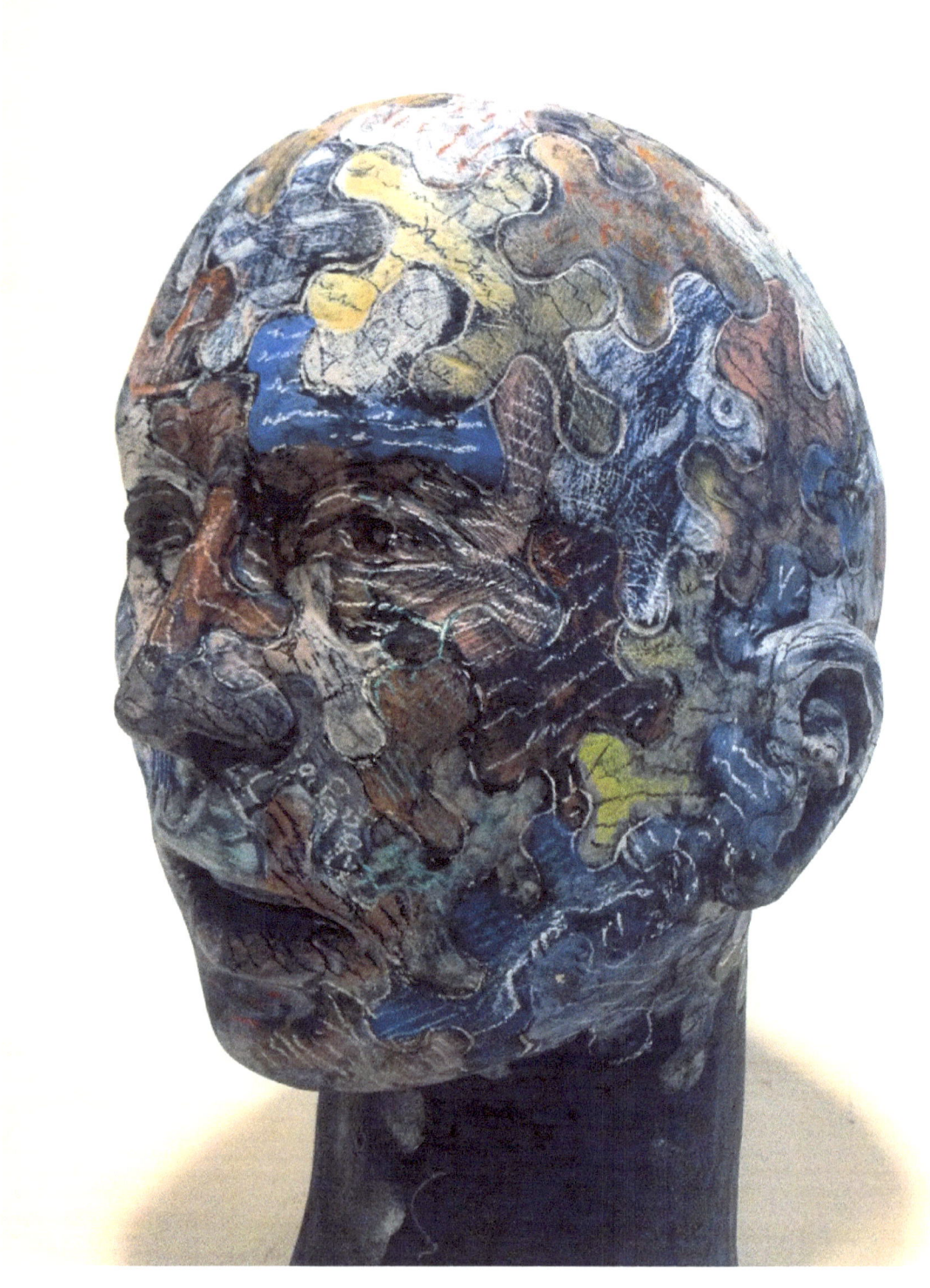

Common identity, polichrome ceramics

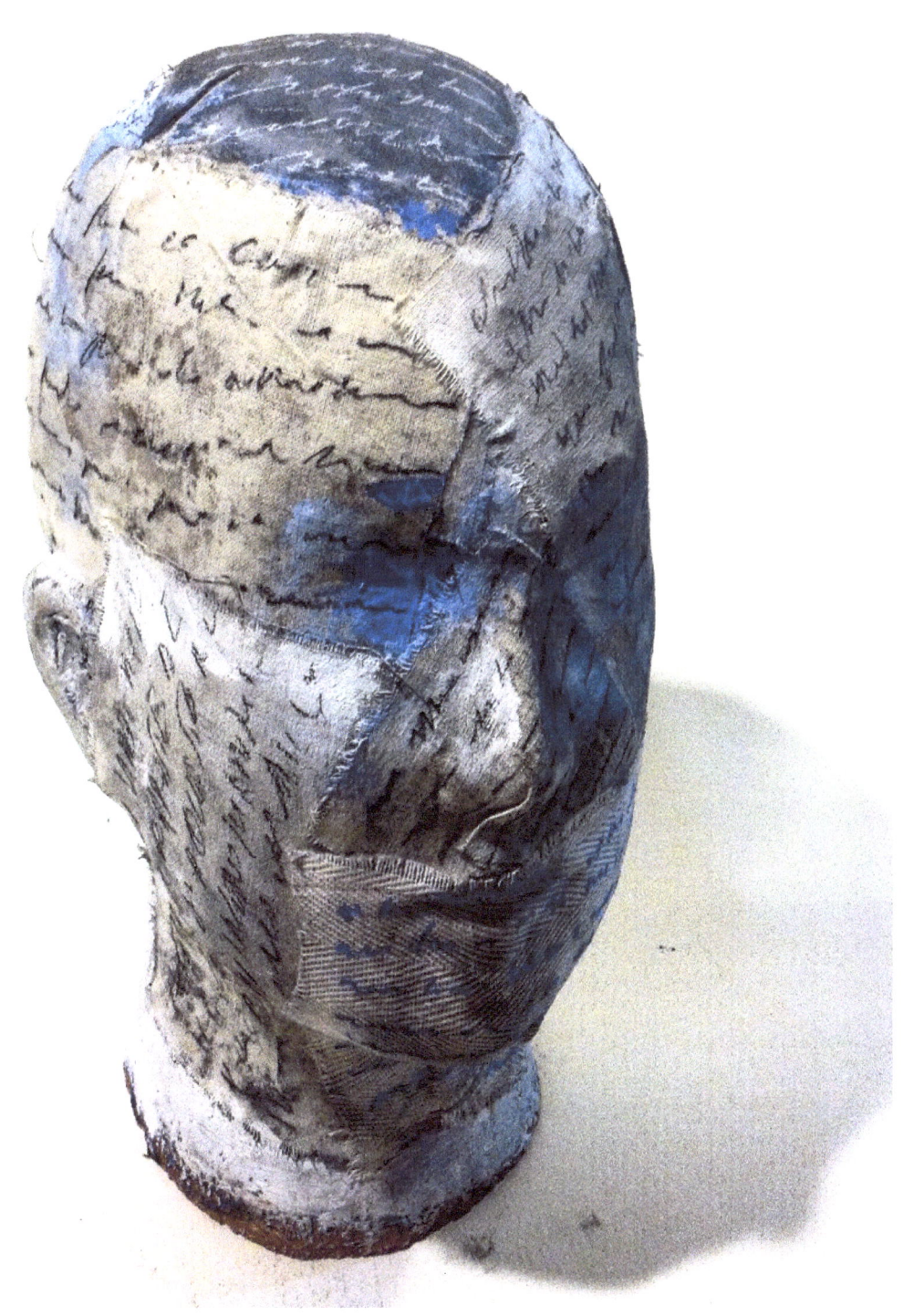

Nothing is written, fabric and gouache on ceramics

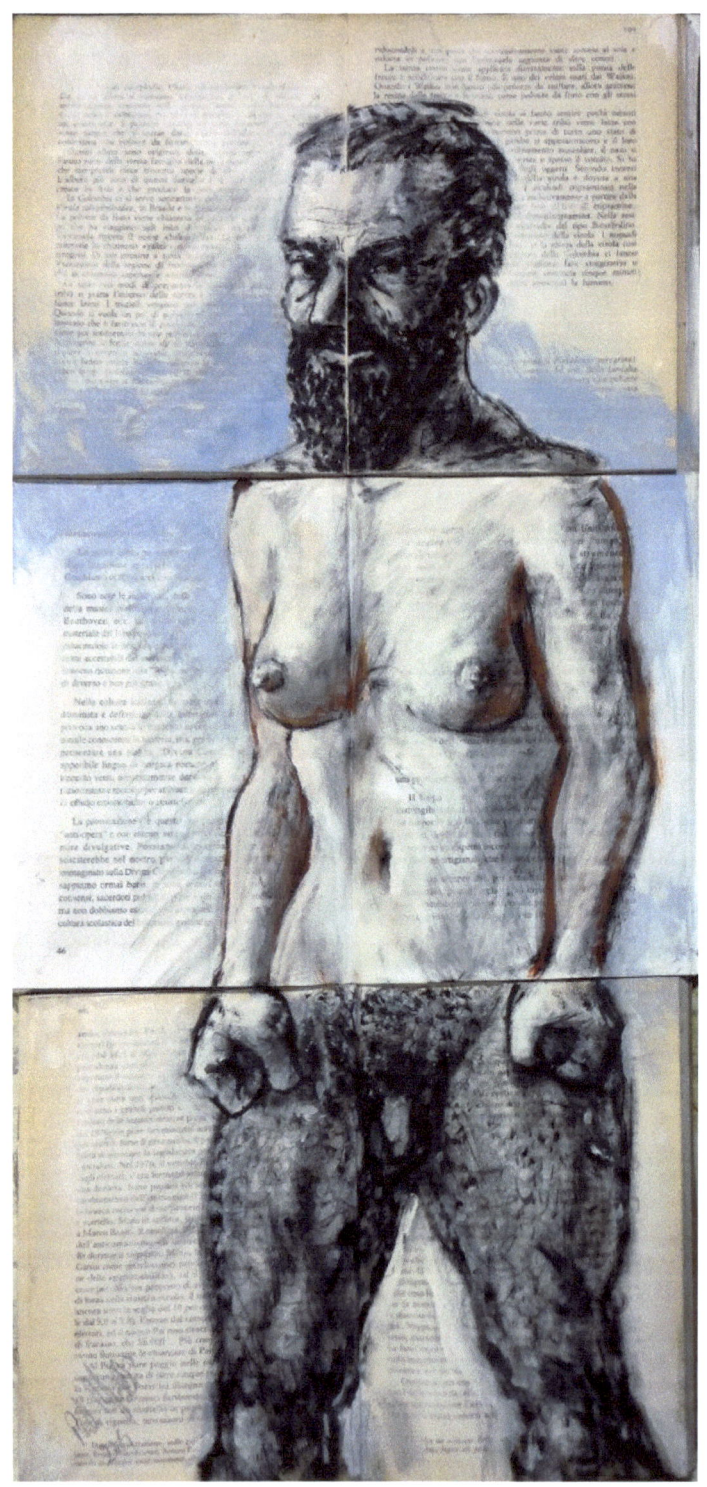

Sexual novel, altered books

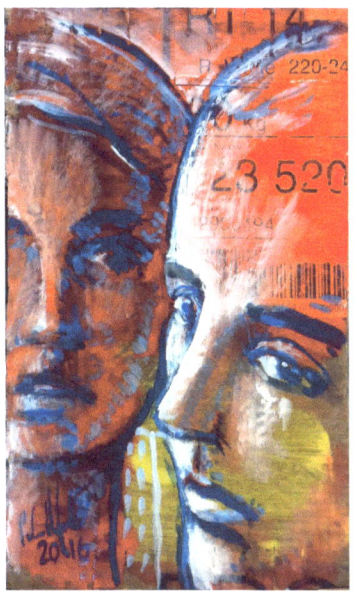

He got numbers, gouache on recycled cardboard

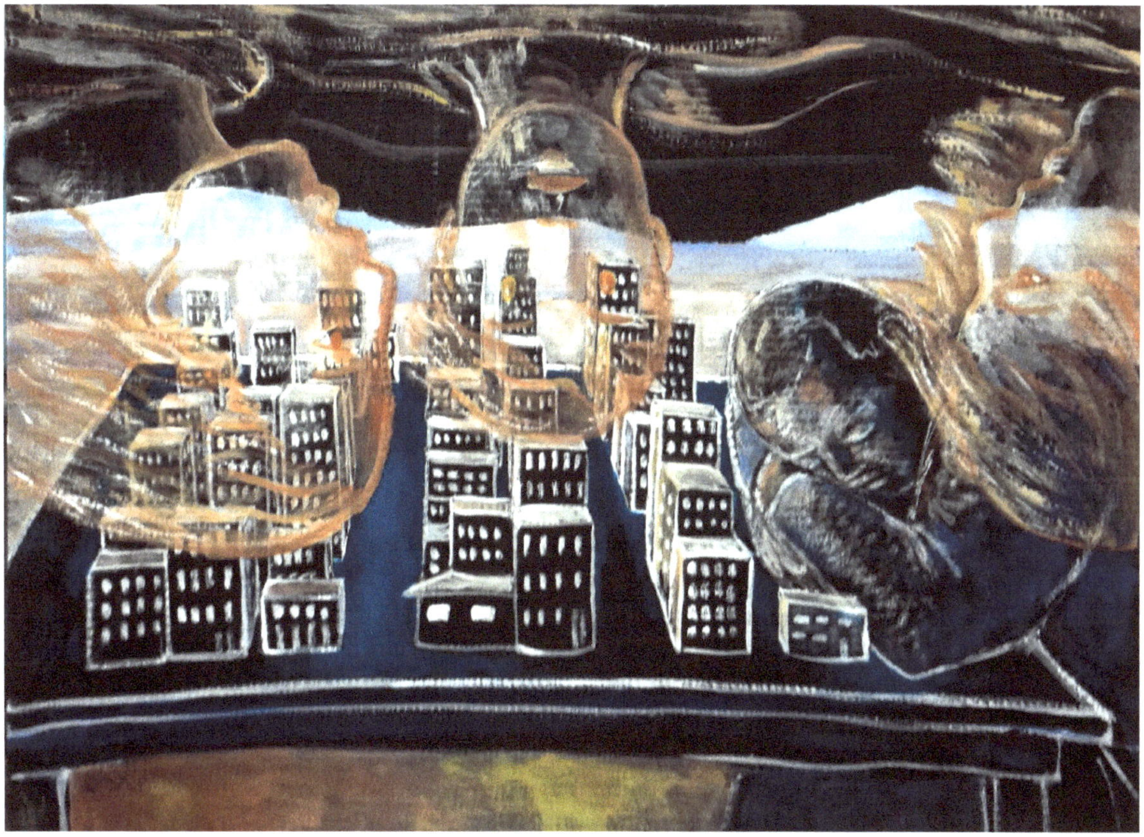

City dreamer, gouache on cardboard

Street Art

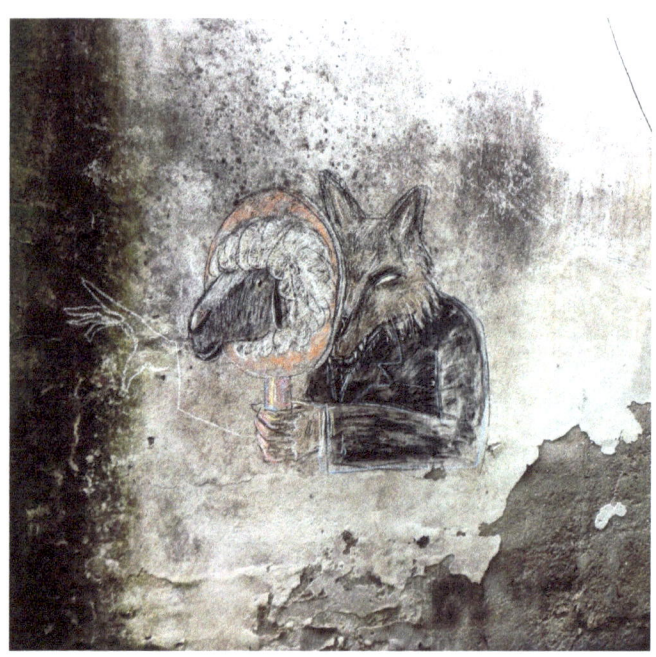

Politician

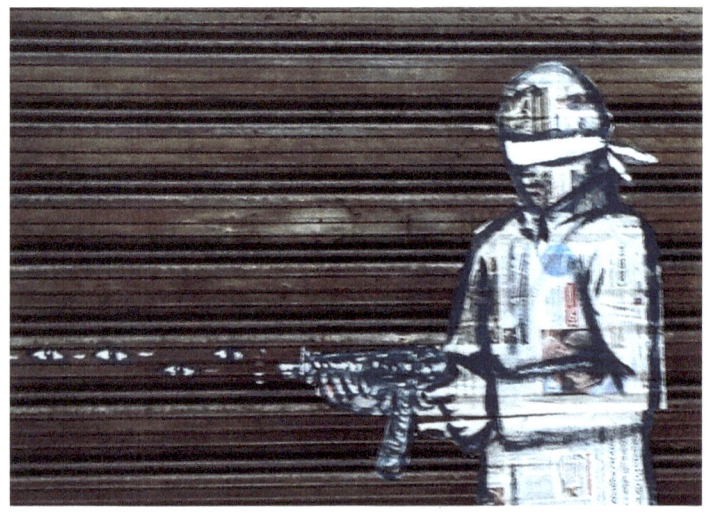

Blind gunman

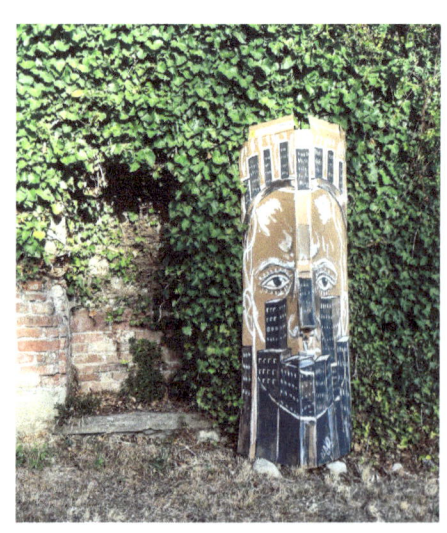

Gatekeeper

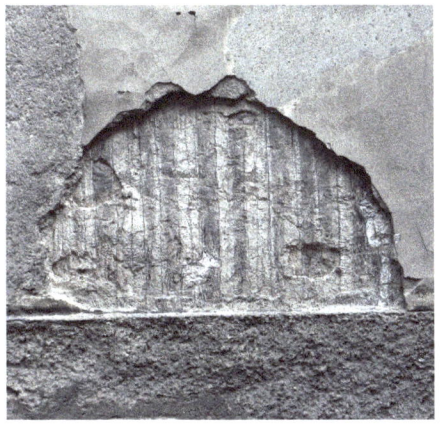

City wood

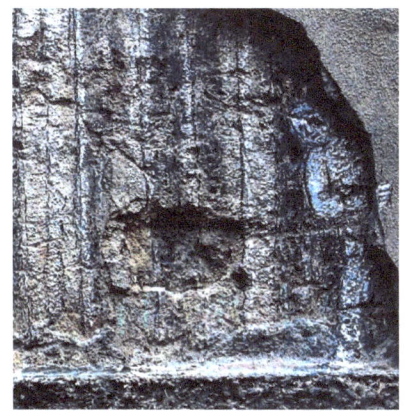

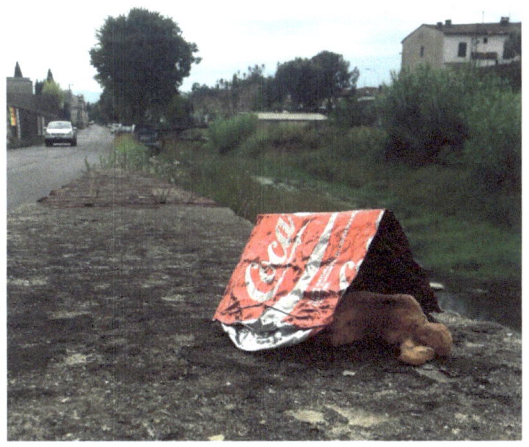

Makeshift tent

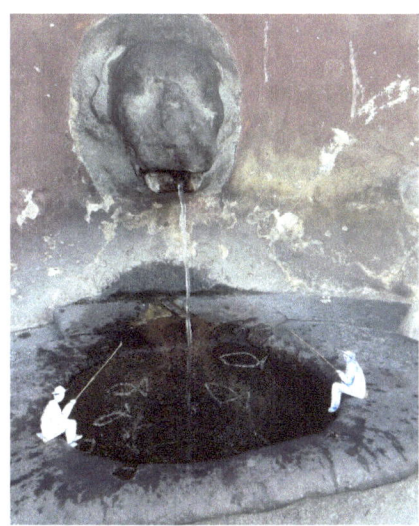

Fishermen

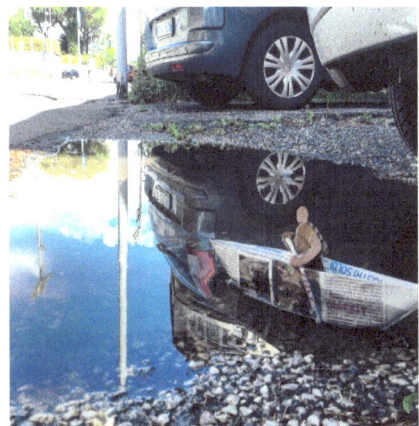

Sailor

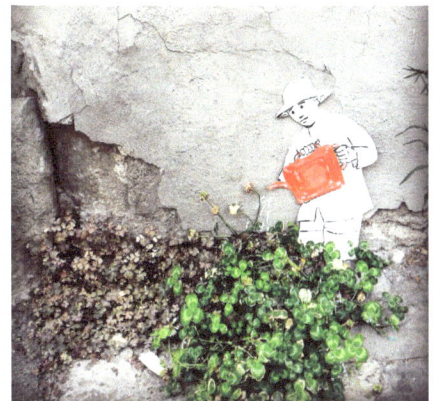

Gardener

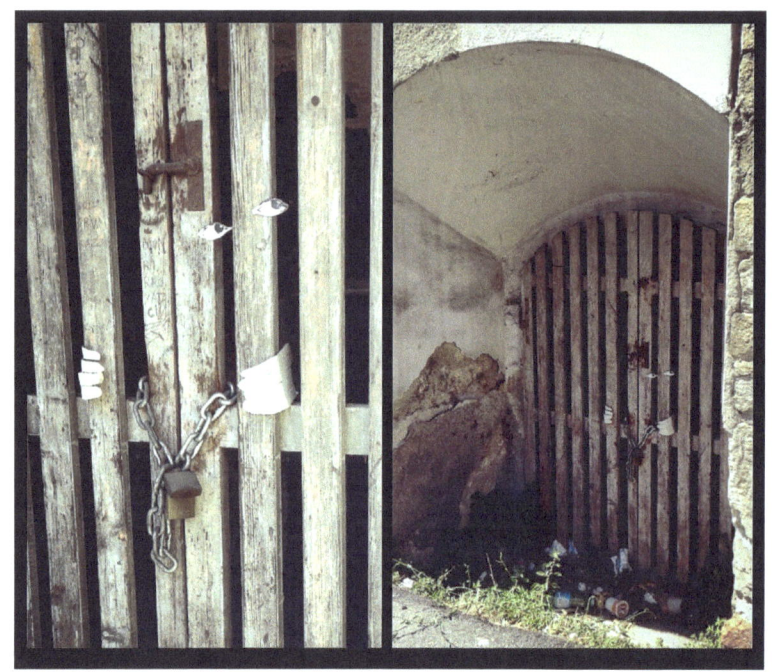

Help!

Fisherman

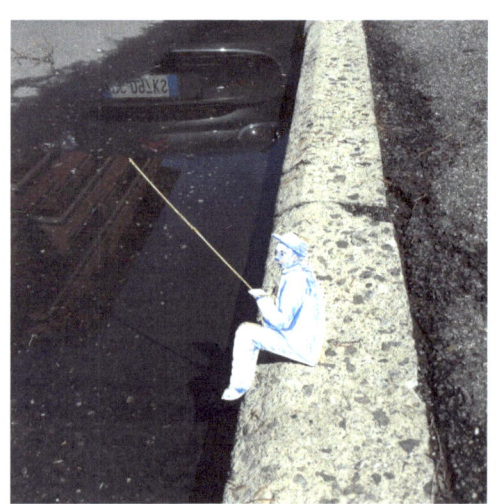

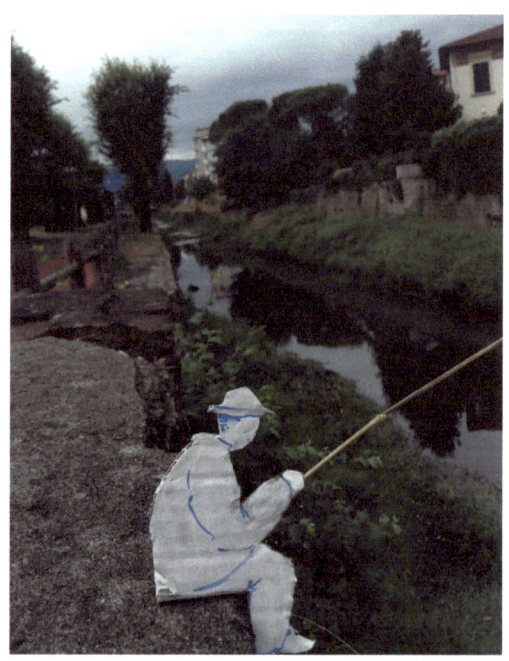

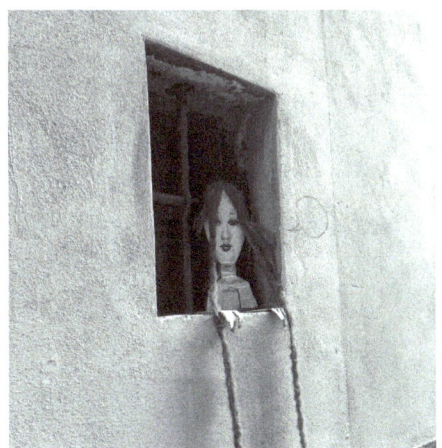

Rapunzel

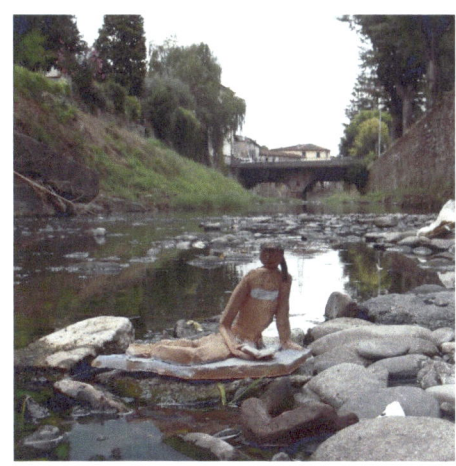

Baigneuse

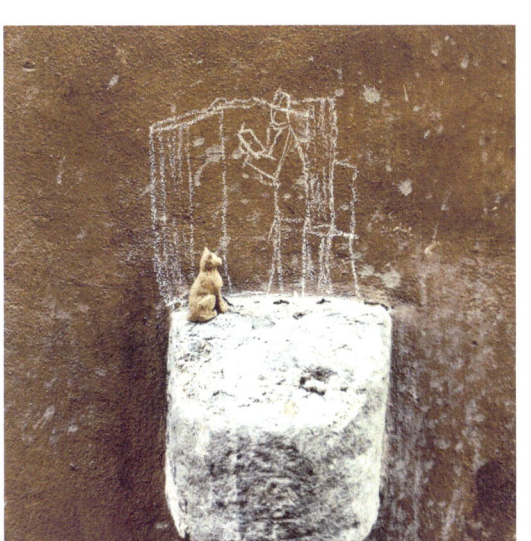

Street cat

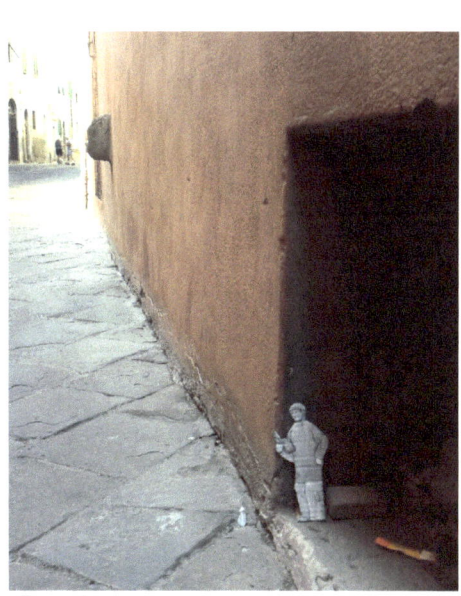

Reader

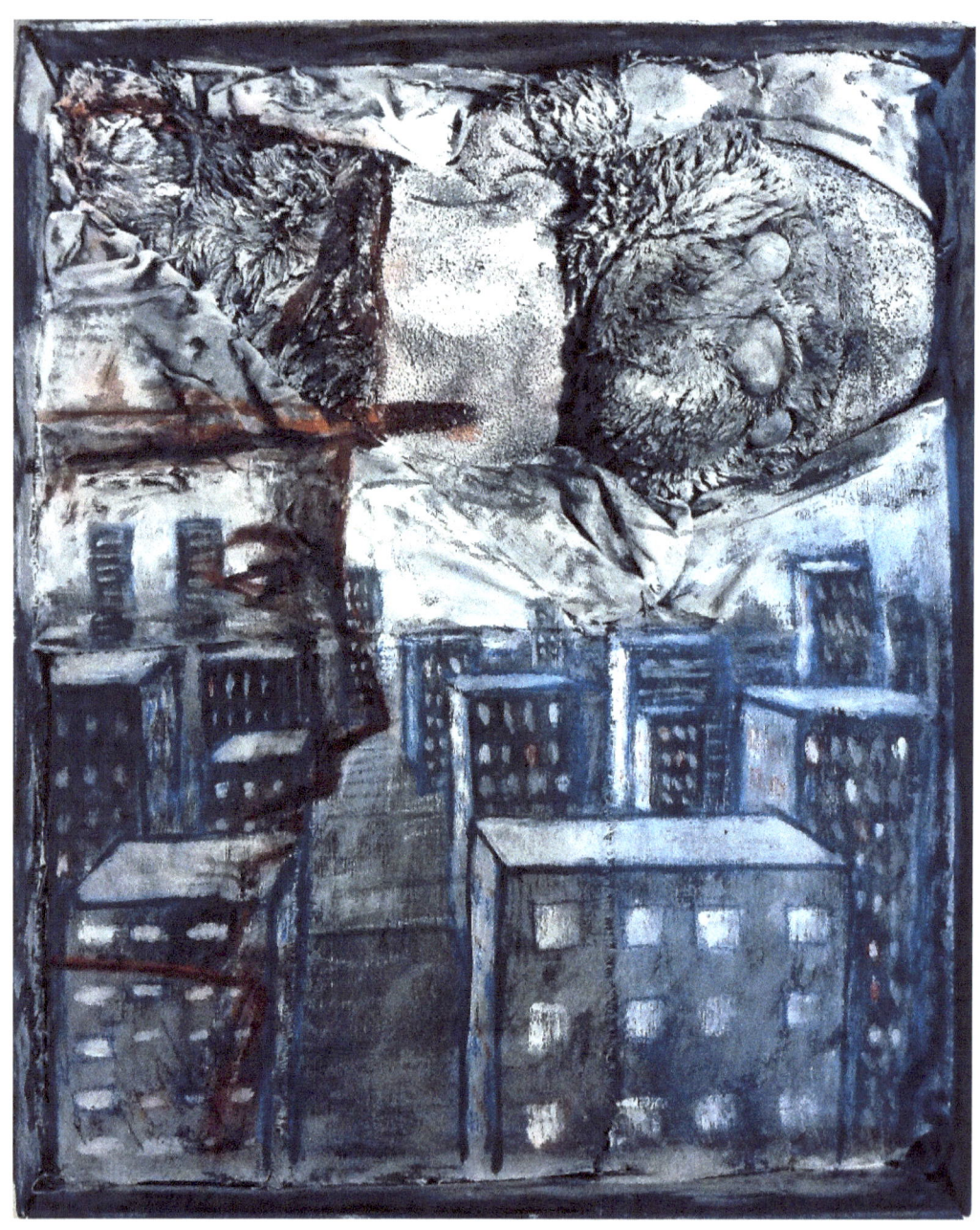

Teddy sky, *mixed technique*

Paolo Beneforti was born 1964 a Pistoia, where he still lives and works.
Self-taught, he achieved many personal and collective exhibitions.
He also teachs Painting, Drawing and Sculpture in his atelier and for public authorities since 1995.

email pbeneforti@gmail.com
personal website www.paolobeneforti.it
twitter: https://twitter.com/paolobitwo
facebook: https://www.facebook.com/paolobenefortiarte
Pinterest: https://www.pinterest.com/paolobitwo/work-of-art/
instagram: https://instagram.com/pbeneforti/

Main solo exhibitions:

2015: La finestra a specchio - Convento di San Domenico, Pistoia
2014: Vati privati - Libreria Les Bouquinistes, Pistoia
2013: Puzzle, città, animali - Conservatorio San Giovanni, Pistoia
2013: Scrittori, giganti, libri, Pistoia - Libreria Les Bouquinistes, Pistoia
2012: Animali - Biblioteca San Giorgio Pistoia
2011: Storie - Biblioteca San Giorgio Pistoia
2009: Galleria Lo Spazio di via dell'Ospizio, Pistoia.
2003: Galleria Alberto Frullini Arte Contemporanea, Pistoia.
2002: Galleria Maniero, Roma
2001: Galleria Alberto Frullini Arte Contemporanea, Pistoia.
2000: Galleria Alberto Frullini Arte Contemporanea, Pistoia.
2000: Mostra Libri illeggibili per lettori inesistenti presso la libreria Cavour di Pistoia.
1997: Salone dell'albergo Le Ondine, Tellaro (La Spezia).
1995: Villa Rospigliosi, Lamporecchio (Pistoia).
1994: Galleria La Spirale, Prato
1993: Villa di Groppoli, Pistoia.
1993   Centro Stranieri di Pistoia, in collaborazione con il gruppo teatrale Gad e la Compagnia di danza Fabula.
1992: Sala Napoleonica del Comune di Pistoia.
1992: Installazione presso la Chiesa di S. Francesco, Pistoia.
1992: Mostra dedicata a Pier Paolo Pasolini presso la Biblioteca di Agliana (Pistoia)

Main collective exhibitions and fairs:

2016: Fusion II, Collective exhibition at Underdog gallery, London
2016: Expo Colectiva Feb 2016, Jorge Miguel Galeria d'Art, Barcelona, Spain
2014: Piccole sculture, grandi maestri - Mostra della collezione Bertini. Fondazione CaRiPT, Palazzo Sozzifanti, Pistoia
2013: Collettiva Associazione Oltre orizzonte, Pistoia
2001: "La fin du livre" Institut franco-japonaise de Tokyo, Tokyo. A cura di Gerard Georges Lemaire
2000: "Colpo di testa" Galleria Maniero, Roma
1999: Artefiera, Bologna
1998: Stand personale alla fiera Etruriarte di Venturina (Livorno).

Fiera di Padova.

1997: Collettiva Galleria Stolz, Massa.

1996: Collettiva Artisti per Fornovolasco, Lucca.
Collettiva dell'Archivio giovani artisti della provincia di Pistoia.

1995: 2a Biennale Arte Pistoiese.

1994: Mostra regionale toscana Arti Figurative, Firenze.
Collettiva Galleria La Spirale, Prato

1993: Biennale Arte Pistoiese.

1992: Premio S. Giorgio, Pistoia.

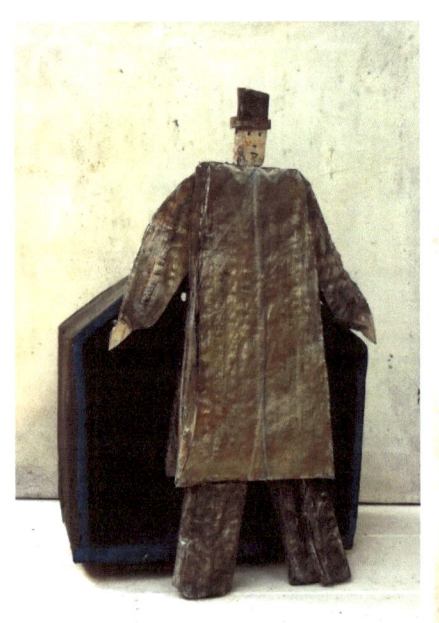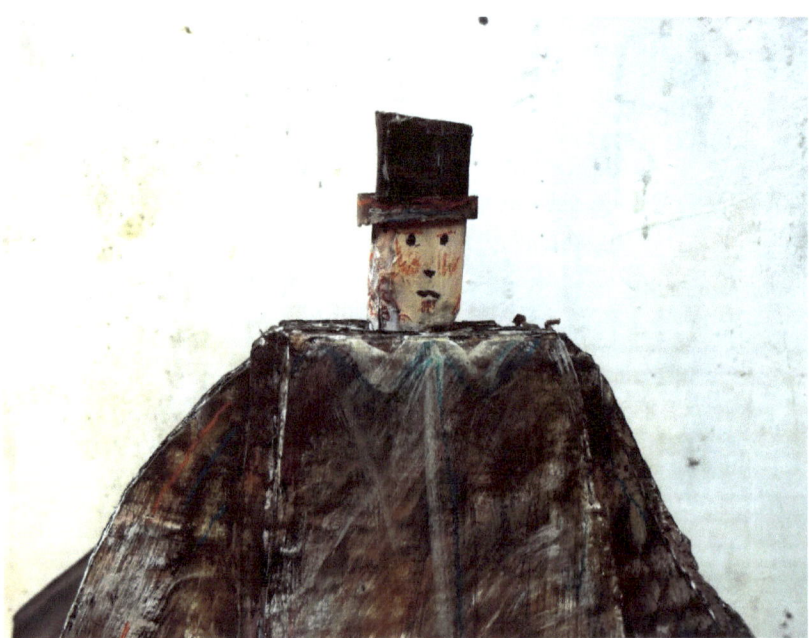

A giant and his house, *Painted cardboard and ceramics*

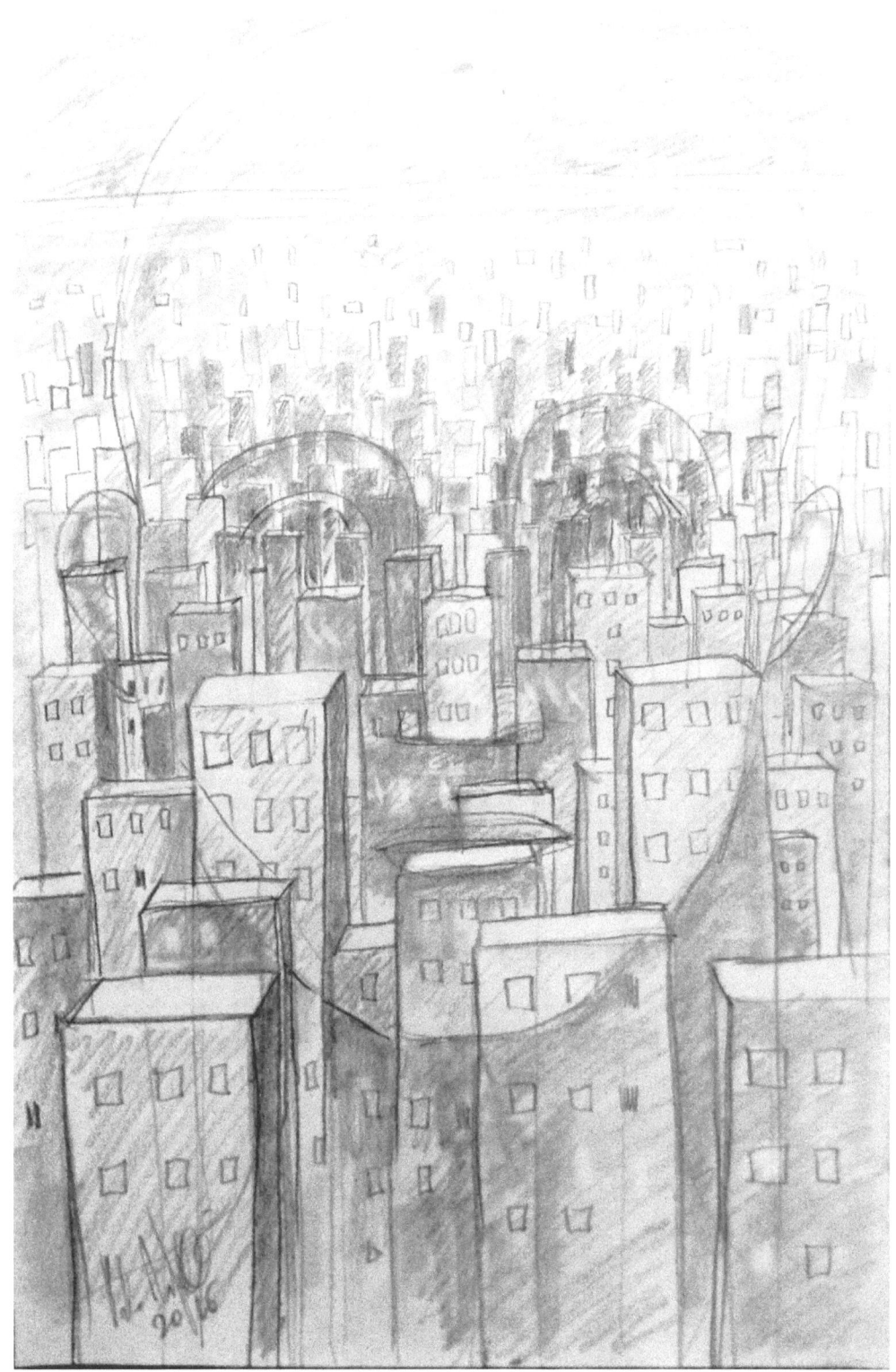

Cityscape, pencil on paper

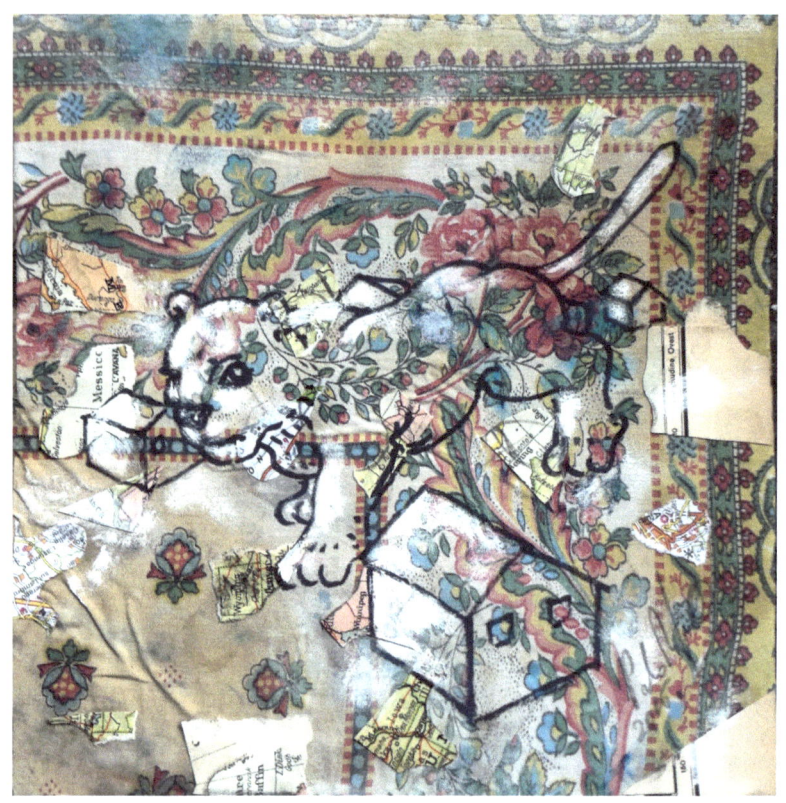

Flowers, collage and gouache on printed fabric

Cover: **Fish hunter**, gouache on crumpled paper, 2016